Recorder from the Beginning

Book 3

John Pitts

Published by
EJA Publications

Exclusive Distributors:

Hal Leonard
7777 West Bluemound Road,
Milwaukee, WI 53213
Email: info@halleonard.com

Hal Leonard Europe Limited
42 Wigmore Street, Marylebone,
London WIU 2 RY
Email: info@halleonardeurope.com

Hal Leonard Australia Pty. Ltd.
4 Lentara Court, Cheltenham,
Victoria 9132, Australia
Email: info@halleonard.com.au

Copyright © 2004 John Pitts.
This book published by Wise Music Group under exclusive licence.

For all works contained herein:
Unauthorized copying, arranging, adapting, recording, Internet posting,
public performance, or other distribution of the music in this publication
is an infringement of copyright. Infringers are liable under the law.

www.halleonard.com

Acknowledgements

Illustrations by Tom Wanless.

Design by Butterworth Design.

Music processing and layout by Camden Music.

This recorder course in three stages has been designed for children aged 7 upwards. Since publication it has become one of the most popular schemes used in many parts of the world.

Recorder from the Beginning assumes no previous knowledge of either music or the recorder, and full explanations are provided at every stage so that specialist teaching is not essential. Teacher's Books are available for each stage, and these contain simple piano accompaniments, guitar chord symbols and suggestions for each tune, often using pitched/unpitched percussion.

All three Pupil's Books are also available in Book & CD editions (CDs not available separately) and the recorded accompaniments will enhance any level of practice or performance, whether by beginners or advanced players. They include a model version of each tune (except in Book 3), followed by exciting, stylish accompaniments for recorders to play along with, both in school and at home.

Revision of the original books for the new full-colour edition has allowed me to make various changes to improve the scheme. The eight extra pages in Book 1 have allowed for some new tunes and rounds, whilst retaining the well-known favourites that have helped to make the scheme such an enduring success. Book 2 has 13 new items as well as new optional duets. Book 3 has the most changes of all, to allow for the introduction of 27 new pieces. I have also made a small change to the order of introducing new notes.

For all these changes in the different books we have recorded exciting new accompaniment tracks for the CDs, plus improved tracks for some of the previous pieces. I have also strengthened and increased the optional opportunities for recorder players to contribute to music units in the National Curriculum, by combining their recorder playing with class music activities such as singing and the use of pitched and unpitched percussion.

I know you will enjoy the lovely pictures created by Tom Wanless, and I wish to thank Tom for his stunning contribution. I also wish to thank my wife Maureen for her never-ending support, help and encouragement over all the years.

I hope the revised edition will be enjoyed as much as the earlier version, and that you will soon have new favourites to add to your present ones.

John Pitts 2004

Contents

Apusski Du (a fishy song)

Zinga-za Samba   Brazilian

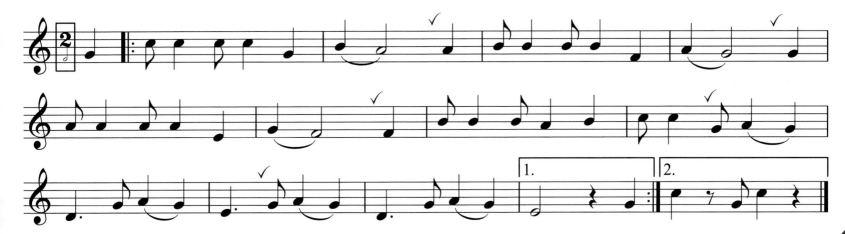

Playing the tied notes

First play this:
Accent note B marked >

Now tie (join together)
both B notes.

Minty's Moody Blues

Fine

D.C. al Fine

In the accompaniment the Da Capo repeat includes the 4 bar introduction not shown here.

Time Signatures

So far we have used time signatures like these: ⟮2⟯ ⟮3⟯ ⟮6⟯

The TOP NUMBER tells us HOW MANY conductor's beats there are in each bar. The NOTE UNDERNEATH shows us HOW MUCH each beat is worth. Now we will use proper time signatures with numbers at the bottom instead of notes.

The BOTTOM NUMBER tells us HOW MUCH each beat is worth. Remember we are counting the conductor's BEATS, not the notes. We can have any number of notes in a bar. But they must add up to the same value as the conductor's beats.

Here are some examples. Try to conduct them while someone else plays the music.
Each of them has three conductor's beats in each bar.

3
2 means that there will be three slow Half Note (½ note) beats (minims) in each bar.
The notes add up to the same value as the conductor's beats.

3
4 means that there will be three Quarter Note (¼ note) beats (crotchets) in each bar.
The notes add up to the same value.

3
8 means that there will be three quick Eighth Note (⅛ note) beats (quavers) in each bar.
The notes add up to the same value.

Old Texas American

All learn Recorder 1 part first. Then split into two groups.
Recorder 2 is the same tune but begins one bar later.
When this happens we call the tune a CANON.
Later, ask some friends to sing the song while you play Recorder 2.

Recorder 1 (or voice)

I'm going to leave_____ old__ Tex - as now,_____ They've got no

Recorder 2

I'm going to leave_____ old__ Tex - as now,_____

use_____ for the long - horn cow._____

___ They've got no use_____ for the long - horn cow._____

Santa Lucia *Neopolitan*

Duet or Solo. The tune is written in the top part all the way through, so can be played solo. When played as a duet the players can change parts at **A** so that each plays some of the main tune.

note B♭

G · B♭

Note B♭ (B flat)

First play note G, then raise your left middle finger. At the same time add on your right hand first finger. Now play note B♭. Before you play the tune practise playing the tied note exercise.

Left

Right

Crombie's Boogie

Playing the tied notes

First play this:
Accent the G marked >

Now join together (tie) both G notes.

Sellinger's Round W. Byrd

See * below

To continue

To end **Fine**

D.C. al Fine

* There are no E♭ notes in this tune, as shown here by the bracket in the Key Signature.

Gavotte Handel

Duet or Solo. The tune is written in the top part all the way through, so can be played solo. When played as a duet the players can change parts at **A** so that each plays some of the main tune.

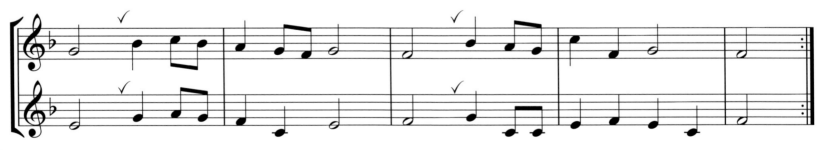

Go Down Moses Spiritual

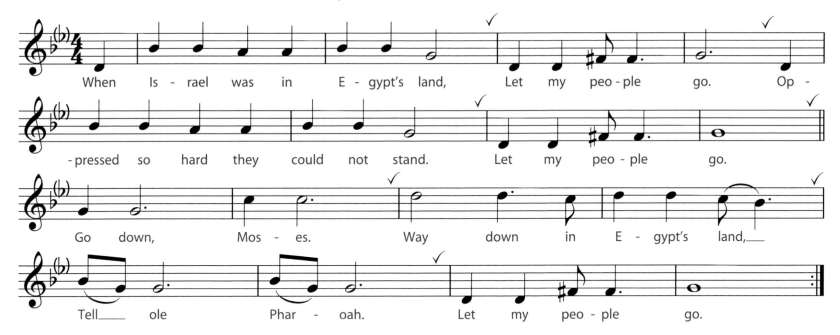

When Is - rael was in E - gypt's land, Let my peo - ple go. Op -
-pressed so hard they could not stand. Let my peo - ple go.
Go down, Mos - es. Way down in E - gypt's land,___
Tell___ ole Phar - oah. Let my peo - ple go.

Cossack Love Song Russian

Slowly

Note G' (upper G)

The fingering is the same as for lower G, except that the left thumb is pinched. Practise changing from lower G to upper G. For G' tongue firmly and use a little more breath pressure.

Left

Right

Star Of County Down Irish

Ade, zur guten Nacht

German

Duet or Solo. The tune is written in the top part all the way through, so can be played solo. When played as a duet the players can change parts at **A** so that each plays some of the main tune.

More use of Upper G (G')

Little David, Play On Your Harp   Spiritual

Introduction: count "1 - 2 - 1"

Trio Mozart

Take care with the staccato and slurred notes.

American Patrol
F.W. Meacham

To continue | To end

Fine

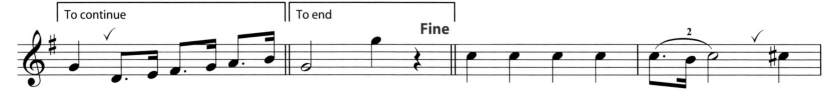

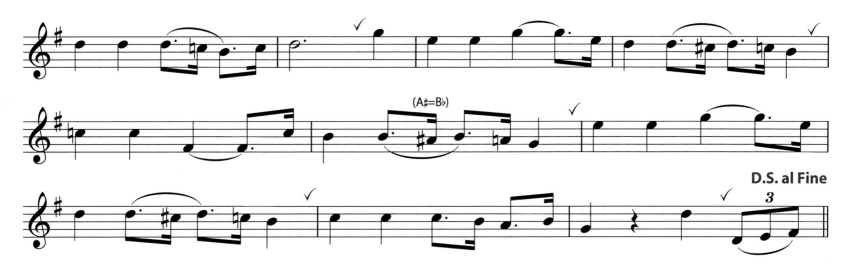

D.S. al Fine

Alternative fingering

Some notes can be fingered in more than one way. This is useful to help play certain slurred notes more smoothly, particularly B - C' and B - D'.

In this tune notes C' - B - C' can be slurred more smoothly if you use the alternative fingering.

Alternative B uses the fingering for note C' plus the 3rd left finger. Suggested places to use alternative fingering are marked 2. Also, make up your own mind!

Try playing this bit of the tune using alternative fingering for note B.

Note F#' (upper F sharp)

First play upper E. Now take off your right first finger.
Do not move any other fingers.
Keep the left thumb pinched.
Now play F#'. Tongue firmly.

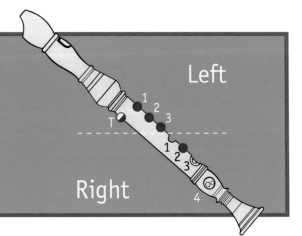

Left

Right

Polka For Paula

Fine

D.C. al Fine

Paddy McGinty's Goat

St Patrick's Day (Irish Jig)

To A Wild Rose

Edward MacDowell

Can you see any parts of this tune that are repeated?
Notice the suggested alternative fingering marked by a '2'.
There is also a duet version of this piece in *Recorder Duets
From The Beginning* **Book 3**.

Rondeau Purcell

The first eight bars of music are repeated at **A** and then again at **C**

Boogie Rock

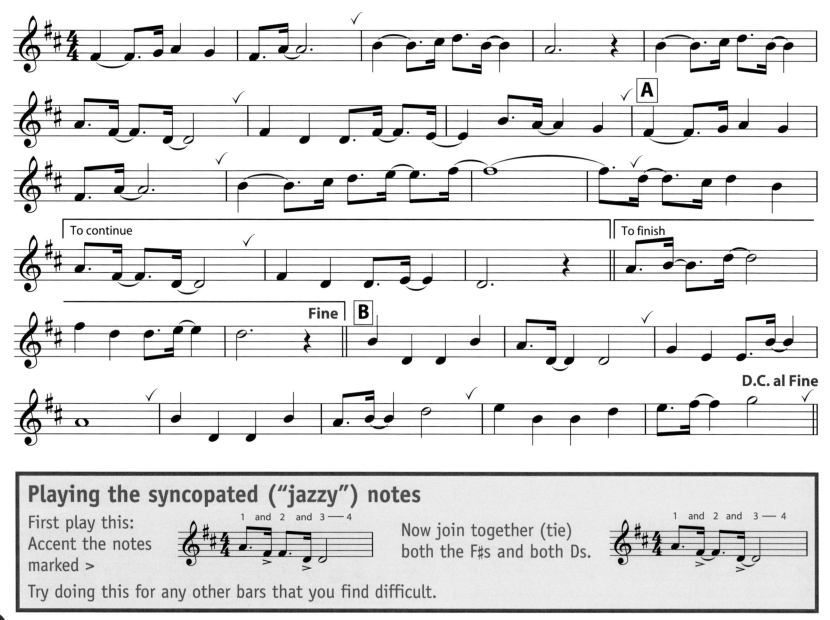

Playing the syncopated ("jazzy") notes

First play this:
Accent the notes marked >

Now join together (tie) both the F♯s and both Ds.

Try doing this for any other bars that you find difficult.

Minuet (from Berenice) Handel

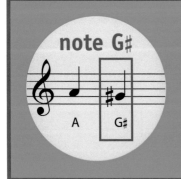

Note G♯ (G sharp)

Play note A. Keep your fingers in position.
Now add on your right hand, first and second
fingers. Look at this diagram to help you.
This is the fingering for note G♯.
Play it.

note G♯

A   G♯

Left

Right

La Cucaracha Mexican Dance

Cudelia Brown

Jamaican Folksong

All learn Recorder 1 part first. Then split into two groups.

Class activity. Ask some friends to sing the song while you play Recorder 2. There are some rumba ostinatos on page 47.

The Lorelei German

Duet or Solo. The tune is written in the top part all the way through, so can be played solo. When played as a duet the players can change parts at **A** so that each plays some of the main tune.

Waikaremoana

New Zealand (Maori)

La Paloma Yradier

This music and Bizet's *Habanera* appear in *Recorder Duets from the Beginning* **Book 3**.

Steady habanera

Voi che sapete Mozart

(from 'The Marriage of Figaro')

note F′

F   F′

Note F′ (upper F)

First play lower F.
Then pinch your left thumb to uncover about
one third of the hole (as for upper E).
At the same time take off your right hand
fourth finger. Tongue firmly.

Left

Right

Tierra Tango

Fine

A

D.C. al Fine

Plaisir d'amour

Martini

Duet or Solo. The tune is written in the top part all the way through, so can be played solo. When played as a duet the players can change parts at **A** so that each plays some of the main tune.

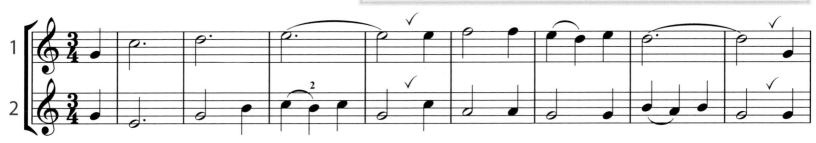

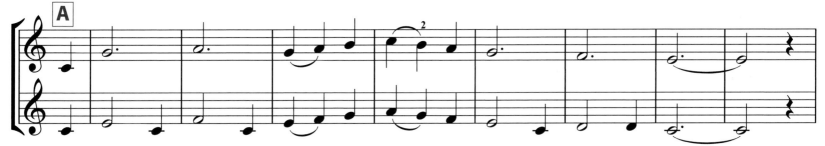

2 = optional alternative fingering

Chiapanecas

Mexican

A duet version of this tune appears in *Recorder From The Beginning* **Around the World.**

Ask a friend to clap in the chorus, where shown in the music.

Auld Lang Syne Scottish

For duets and other tunes using note F see *Recorder Duets from the Beginning* **Books 2 and 3.**

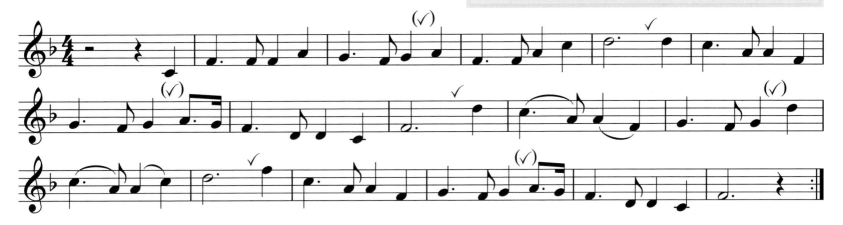

The Swazi Warrior African

Note D#′ (upper D sharp)
Note E♭′ (upper E flat)

Both notes sound the same and use the same fingering. Play upper D. Keep your fingers in position. Now add your third left finger and the first three fingers on your right hand. This leaves the top and bottom holes uncovered at the front, also the back thumb hole uncovered.

notes D#′ & E♭′

D′ D#′ E♭′

Left

Right

Weeping Willow

A Ragtime Two Step by Scott Joplin

Note D#′ appears three times in this tune.
Can you see where?

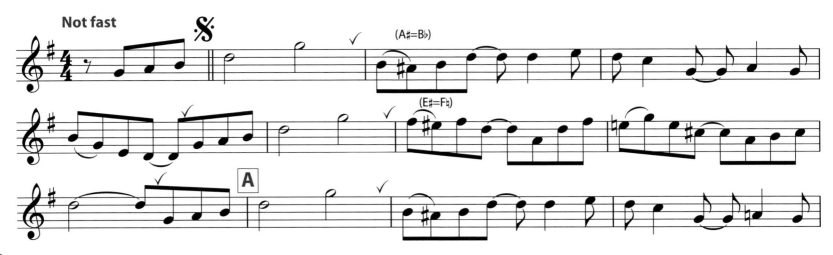

Fine **B**

C

D.S. al Fine

This piece appears in *Recorder From The Beginning* **Blues, Rags and Boogies**

notes D♯ & E♭

Note E♭ (lower E flat)
Note D♯ (lower D sharp)
Both notes sound the same and use the same fingering. Play note D. Now slide your right hand third finger a little to the right. This uncovers the smaller first hole.
This is the fingering for E♭ or D♯. Play it.

Left

Right

El Choclo Argentinean

Note E♭ only appears twice in this tune. Where?

Ask a friend to play the first rhythm on either claves or castanets to accompany the tango.

Another friend could play the second rhythm on a tambourine or jingle ring.

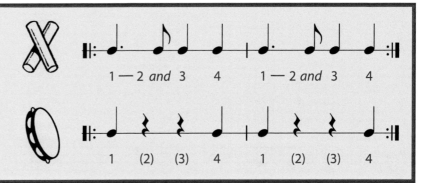

1 — 2 *and* 3   4   1 — 2 *and* 3   4

1   (2)   (3)   4   1   (2)   (3)   4

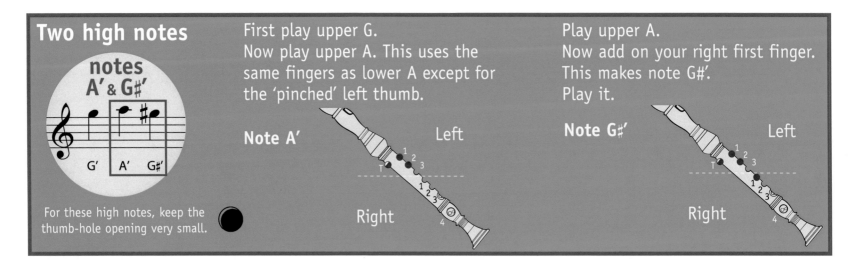

Two high notes

notes A' & G#'

G' A' G#'

For these high notes, keep the thumb-hole opening very small.

First play upper G.
Now play upper A. This uses the same fingers as lower A except for the 'pinched' left thumb.

Note A'

Left

Right

Play upper A.
Now add on your right first finger. This makes note G#'.
Play it.

Note G#'

Left

Right

Orljak Tango (pronounce "j" as "y")

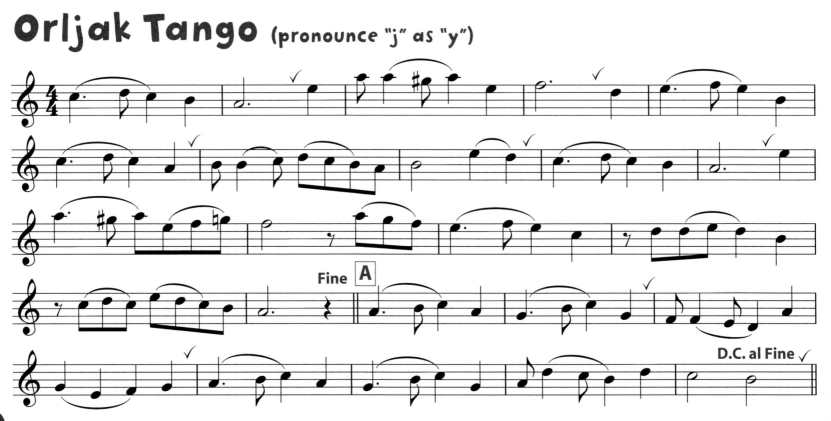

Fine **A**

D.C. al Fine ✓

O Sole Mio

Music by Eduardo di Capua, words by Giovanni Capurro

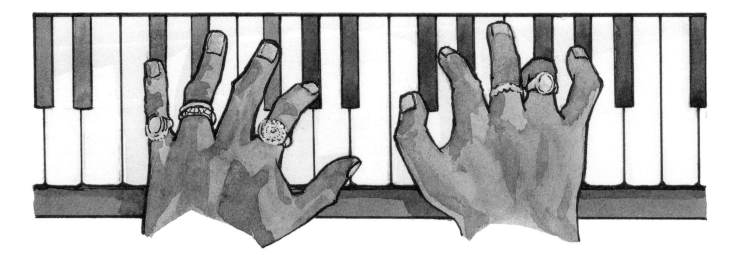

Peacherine Rag Scott Joplin

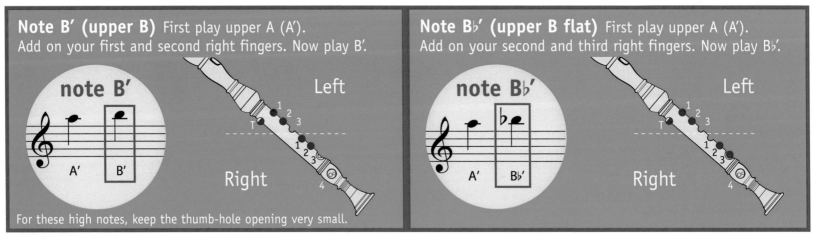

Note B' (upper B) First play upper A (A').
Add on your first and second right fingers. Now play B'.

note B'

A' | B'

Left

Right

For these high notes, keep the thumb-hole opening very small.

Note B♭' (upper B flat) First play upper A (A').
Add on your second and third right fingers. Now play B♭'.

note B♭'

A' | B♭'

Left

Right

Minuet Purcell

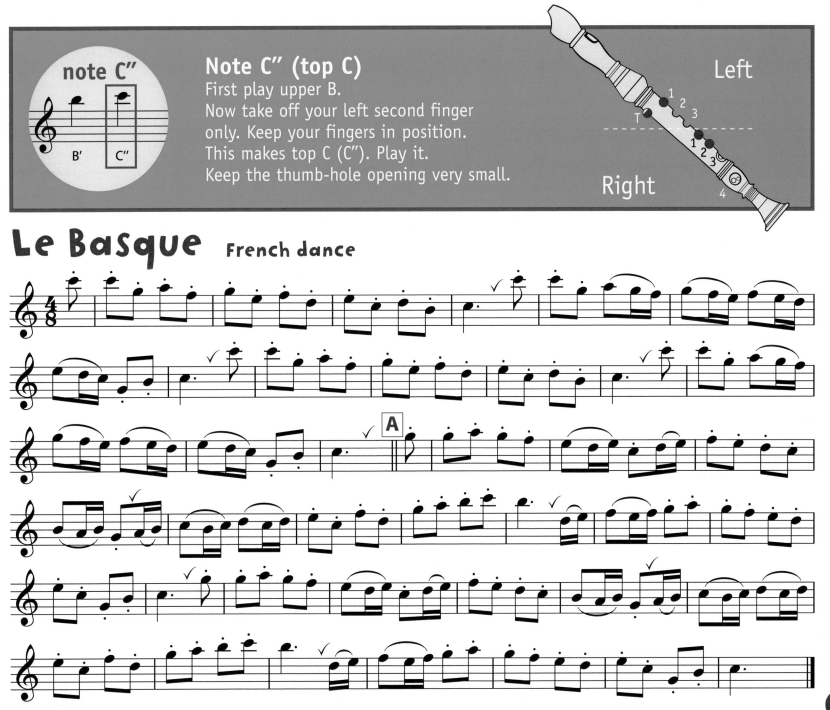

Palmarito Rumba

Quite steadily

The **rumba** is a Cuban dance which uses a syncopated rhythm pattern. An important characteristic is the anticipation of the second beat in the bass of each bar, resulting in this subdivision:

Claves can play this rhythm as an effective accompaniment.
An easier way to count it is as follows:

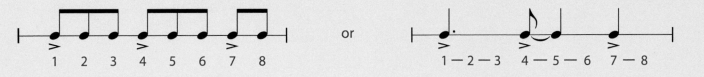

In addition to the basic rhythm of the bass line, accompaniment chords usually fill in all the quavers not played by the bass, as used in the piano accompaniment in the Teacher's Book.

CD Book 3

The CD provides exciting and lively accompaniments, which will give pleasure in the practice and performance of even the simplest of tunes.

Each piece begins with an introduction. Where a tune is repeated, the introduction recurs as a link to the second accompanied playing. The music is arranged so that the tune can still clearly be heard by recorder players playing along with the CD.

Backing tracks arranged by CN Productions.
Voice-over by John Pitts.
CD recorded, mixed and mastered by Jonas Persson and Neil Williams.

CD Track Listing

1   Tuning note A
2   Duerme Niño, Pequeñito
3   Apusski du
4   Zinga-za Samba
5   Minty's Moody Blues
6   Old Texas
7   Santa Lucia
8   Crombie's Boogie
9   Sellinger's Round
10 Gavotte (Handel)
11 Go Down Moses
12 Cossack Love Song
13 Star Of County Down
14 Ade, zur guten Nacht
15 Little David, Play On Your Harp
16 Trio (Mozart)
17 American Patrol
18 Polka for Paula
19 Paddy McGinty's Goat
20 St Patrick's Day
21 To A Wild Rose
22 Rondeau (Purcell)
23 Boogie Rock
24 Minuet from 'Berenice' (Handel)
25 La Cucaracha
26 Cudelia Brown
27 The Lorelei
28 Waikaremoana
29 La Paloma
30 Voi che sapete (Mozart)
31 Tierra Tango
32 Plaisir d'amour
33 Chiapanecas
34 Auld Lang Syne
35 The Swazi Warrior
36 Weeping Willow (Joplin)
37 El Choclo
38 Orljak Tango
39 O Sole Mio
40 Peacherine Rag (Joplin)
41 Minuet (Purcell)
42 Le Basque
43 Palmarito Rumba

The CD accompaniments begin with an introduction, although this is not shown in the Pupil's music. Where a tune is repeated, the introduction is also repeated.

To remove your CD from the plastic sleeve, lift the small lip on the side to break the perforated flap. Replace the disc after use for convenient storage.